Compliments of

Lafayette
Convention & Visitors Commission
(337) 232-3737 • (800) 346-1958 • www.lafayettetravel.com

NASCAR COOKS

WITH TABASCO® BRAND PEPPER SAUCE

Celebrating NASCAR's 50th Anniversary.

Featuring the hottest collection of

favorite recipes from 50 NASCAR celebrities!

HarperCollins*Publishers*

NASCAR COOKS was published by HarperCollins*Publishers* Inc.,
10 East 53rd Street, New York, NY 10022. Senior Vice President and Publishing Director: John Silbersack; Senior Vice President Finance and Operations: Ken Fund; Vice President and Director of HarperCollins Enterprises: Frank Fochetta; Director of Brand Publishing: Patricia Teberg; Marketing Director: Amy Wasserman; Production Director: Dianne Walber.

NASCAR COOKS was designed, produced, and coordinated by RDM/Hone Visual Communications, Philadelphia, 800-765-7685. Food Photography: Stephen Hone, RDM/Hone; Project Coordinator: Clare Hone; Food Stylist: Debbie Wahl; Food Editor: Sandra Day; NASCAR Photography: Phil Cavelli, Jim Fluharty, Tim Wilcox, Elmer Cappell, Landon George, Don Winchester, Don Grassman, Ernie Masche, Daytona Racing Archive. TABASCO Photography: TABASCO Photo Archive.

The TEAM TABASCO® No. 35 Pontiac Grand Prix was designed by Sam Bass of Sam Bass Illustrations.

With special thanks to key individuals at NASCAR and TABASCO for their contributions in the creation of *NASCAR COOKS*: Director of Special Projects & Publishing, NASCAR: Paul Brooks; Editorial Manager, NASCAR: Kelly Crouch; Director of Operations, NASCAR: Kevin Triplett; Vice President Marketing, TABASCO: Martin Manion; Marketing Manager, TABASCO: Donna Betzer; V.P. Sports & Entertainment Marketing, Kragie Newell Agency/Atlanta: Claudia Cahill.

NASCAR® is a registered trademark of NASCAR, Inc., Daytona Beach, FL 32114. www.nascar.com

TABASCO® is a registered trademark and servicemark exclusively of McIlhenny Company, Avery Island, LA 70513.

HarperCollins books may be purchased for education, business, or sales promotional use. For information please write: Special Markets Department, HarperCollins*Publishers* Inc., 10 East 53rd Street, New York, NY 10022.

FIRST EDITION
ISBN 0-06-105066-0
98 99 00 01 02 WCR 10 9 8 7 6 5 4 3 2 1

CONTENTS

Deep within the bayous and marshes of South Louisiana's Gulf Coast lies a subterranean "iceberg of salt" surrounded by these wetlands. Still owned by direct descendants of the Avery family, Avery Island is home to wildlife, exotic flora, rich oil deposits, salt, and a product respected throughout the world: TABASCO® brand Pepper Sauce.

With its bold, fiery taste, TABASCO® Sauce was first produced by Edmund McIlhenny in 1868. McIlhenny, a gourmet in his own right, discovered that the rich fields of the Island would cultivate the finest red peppers. Crushing selected red peppers with native Avery Island salt, a special mash resulted. This mixture was then placed in oak barrels to age. Later, the fully aged pepper mash was skillfully blended with distilled natural vinegar, strained, packaged, and shipped to clubs, restaurants, and wholesale grocers.

Today, TABASCO® Sauce—a natural recipe that has never changed—is still revered for its distinctive, piquant flavor and remarkable versatility. From home kitchens to tailgate parties to your favorite restaurants, people crave the unique and tasty "heat" that TABASCO® brand Pepper Sauce adds to all kinds of food.

The McIlhenny family is now thrilled to bring that same energy and excitement to TEAM TABASCO®, a red-hot entry into the NASCAR Winston Cup Series, with Todd Bodine at the wheel. Like the McIlhennys, Todd comes from a family that's rich in tradition. Brothers Geoff and Brett Bodine are NASCAR Winston Cup Series veterans. A race car driver for 15 years, Todd most recently competed in the NASCAR

Busch Series, Grand National Division. In the last three years alone, he captured seven wins, 27 top-five finishes, and 47 top-ten finishes in that circuit.

Just as TEAM TABASCO® is gearing up to add even more heat to America's hottest sport, the McIlhenny family takes great pride in teaming up with yet another fine family, the Frances, owners of NASCAR, in celebrating the 50th Anniversary of NASCAR in 1998—and bringing you this exclusive collection of recipes from NASCAR drivers and other NASCAR celebrities.

Now, ladies and gentlemen, start your…ovens, ranges, and barbeque grills!

NASCAR COOKS will bring *your family* years of great food and great times!

It starts out as a quiet Sunday afternoon. Around the country, millions of eager fans wait in anticipation as world-class athletes climb into their stout racing machines waiting for that famous charge: "Gentlemen, start your engines!"

Seconds later the roar of engines is heard all over the country. NASCAR is a sport as unique as both its participants and its fans. It's a sport defined by tradition, passion, and cama-raderie—guided by the wisdom and vision of one man, William Henry Getty "Bill" France, Sr.

Official NASCAR pace car kicking off Speed Week, Daytona Beach 1950

Bill and Anne France, Sr., Daytona Beach 1939.

"Big Bill," who had been promoting stock car racing in Daytona Beach, Florida, gathered drivers, noted mechanics, and promoters together on December 14, 1947. His mission: to set fundamental guidelines and bylaws for stock car racing everywhere. They called the new organiza-tion NASCAR, the National Association of Stock Car Auto Racing, and dedicated it to setting the highest safety, ethical, and racing standards, strengthening its own reputation for being as good as its word.

Today, the cars are faster and the speedways larger, but the thousands of drivers and their loyal crews are the same polished professionals revered for their strategy, teamwork, skill, and plain old-fashioned grit. They are new heroes of the American road in a sport that spans generations.

Flagman, Daytona Beach- Road Course, Daytona Beach.

NASCAR is indeed unique. It is a sport in which fathers and sons, brothers and neighbors, turn from intense competitors and fierce adversaries, after the green flag is dropped, to proud and admiring compatriots when the checkered flag waves the winner into Victory Lane.

The NASCAR family is proud not only of their heritage but of the dedicated fans who share the same spirit with the drivers, their families, and the "weekend warriors" who make each event memorable. Together, they take pride in the true American spirit of competition and sportsmanship, envisioned by Bill France over 50 years ago in Daytona Beach.

Start your engines! Join in the celebration of NASCAR'S 50th Anniversary. It'll be a wonderful ride for everyone!

50TH ANNIVERSARY
1948 · 1998
50
NASCAR

START YOUR ENGINES

The crowd anxiously awaits this ceremonial command.
The drivers fire their engines and pull onto the track.

BILL FRANCE'S "PERFECT HOT DOG"

"Pulliams' Barbecue in Winston-Salem, North Carolina, has the best hot dogs imaginable. I follow their recipe whenever I make hot dogs at home, and it goes like this: Cook the hot dog in a fry pan on top of the stove in just a small amount of margarine or bacon fat. While the hot dog is frying, place the hot dog bun on a hot, buttered grill to brown. The secret here is not to open up the bun where sliced, but to grill it closed-slit side on the grill, so that only the slit side of the bun is grilled. When the hot dog and bun are cooked, add mustard, Garden Cole Slaw, and TABASCO® Sauce."

BILL FRANCE'S GARDEN COLE SLAW

1/2	cup mayonnaise
2	tablespoons honey
2	tablespoons lemon juice
1 1/2	teaspoons TABASCO® brand Green Pepper Sauce
1/2	teaspoon salt
1/2	teaspoon ground ginger
4	cups shredded cabbage
1	medium green or red bell pepper, chopped
1	medium carrot, shredded
1	medium zucchini, shredded
1/4	cup chopped green onion

In a large bowl, combine mayonnaise, honey, lemon juice, TABASCO® Sauce, salt, and ginger until blended. Add cabbage, bell pepper, carrot, zucchini, and green onion; toss to coat well. Cover and refrigerate at least 2 hours to blend flavors. Makes 6 servings.

He raced into more than just the legacy founded by his father Bill France, Sr. Bill Jr. has helped steer NASCAR into America's fastest-growing sport. Nowhere in history has one sport grown so fast, with fans so loyal.

From collecting tickets to selling sodas and hot dogs at races as a youth to serving as NASCAR's president for the last 26 years, Bill has worked in

every aspect of the sport. He is fiercely dedicated to making NASCAR the finest sport in America—guiding rules, regulations, and its growing membership with the same spirit as his father.

So it should come as no surprise that Bill and his wife Betty Jane's specialty is the all-American "Perfect Hot Dog" served with spicy Garden Cole Slaw.

France-style, of course!

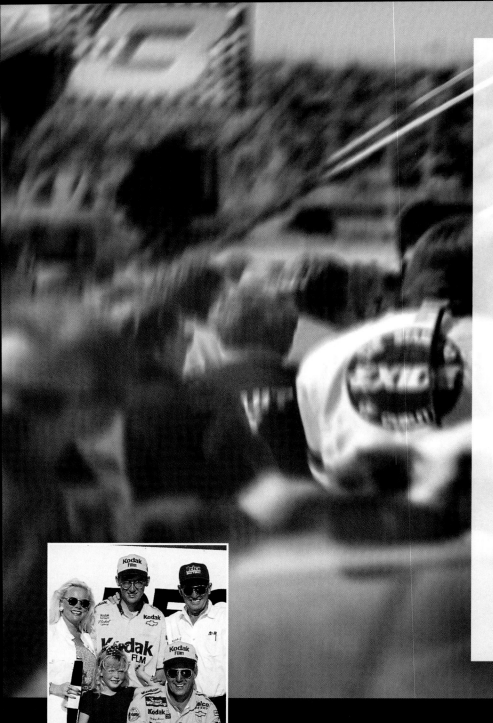

Sterling Marlin's Tuscan Summer Salad

1/4 cup olive oil

3 tablespoons balsamic vinegar

1 garlic clove, crushed

1 teaspoon salt

1 teaspoon TABASCO® brand Pepper Sauce

1 small loaf coarse Italian bread, stale

3 large ripe tomatoes, cut into large chunks

1 large red onion, cut in half and sliced

1 large cucumber, cut into large chunks

1 large red bell pepper, cut into large pieces

1 large yellow bell pepper, cut into large pieces

1 cup arugula leaves

1/2 cup fresh basil leaves

1/2 cup black olives

1 tablespoon capers

In a small bowl, combine olive oil, balsamic vinegar, garlic, salt, and TABASCO® Sauce; set aside. In a large bowl, tear bread into large pieces to make about 4 cups. Add tomatoes, onion, cucumber, bell peppers, arugula, basil, olives, and capers; pour vinaigrette over top and mix well. Let stand 30 minutes before serving. Makes 4 servings.

Calm, cool, courageous, and collected. Sterling Marlin's steady drive and determination have earned him quite a reputation. He won the prestigious Daytona 500 in 1994 and then went back the next year to win it again—becoming only the third man in history to do so!

Sterling owes a lot to his father, Coo Coo, who was a successful NASCAR

driver in his own right. His dad started him out in his pit crew back in his home state of Tennessee. Eight years later, Sterling was named the NASCAR Winston Cup Series Rookie of the Year. From there, he's won 6 races and over $10 million.

The Marlin family—his wife, Paula, and two kids, Steadman and Sutherlin—still call Tennessee home. And they hope you'll feel right at home serving their Tuscan Summer Salad.

Jeff Gordon's Mediterranean Chicken Salad

1 tablespoon chopped onion

1½ teaspoons minced garlic

½ teaspoon salt, divided

½ cup olive oil, divided

¼ teaspoon TABASCO® brand Pepper Sauce

2 cups diced cooked chicken breast

1 medium tomato, diced

6 pitted black olives

1 tablespoon thinly sliced sun-dried tomato

6 mushrooms, sliced

4 fresh basil leaves, chopped

1 head romaine lettuce, washed and dried

2 tablespoons balsamic vinegar

Combine onion and garlic in a small bowl; sprinkle with half of salt and mash into a semi-paste. Add remaining salt, ¼ cup of olive oil, and TABASCO® Sauce; mix well. In a medium bowl, combine chicken, diced tomato, olives, sun-dried tomato, mushrooms, and basil; pour olive oil mixture over top and toss to coat well. Slice romaine crosswise into 1-inch-wide strips and place in a large bowl. In a small bowl, whisk together balsamic vinegar and remaining ¼ cup olive oil and pour over lettuce; toss to coat well and arrange on two plates. Spoon chicken mixture on top. Makes 2 servings.

If there's a recipe for a new racing hero, then Jeff Gordon has all the ingredients! He was five years old when he started wheeling quarter midgets in Vallejo, California. And his torrid pursuit spirited him to be the youngest driver to win a qualifying race for the Daytona 500.

His rare combination of maturity and aggressiveness earned him a win at

the Brickyard 400 at age 23. And NASCAR Winston Cup championships in 1995 and 1997, make him, at 26, the youngest two-time champion in NASCAR history.

Gordon's winning streak is as captivating as the winning smile he flashes at every race. His Mediterranean Chicken Salad is guaranteed to bring a smile to his many fans.

Randy LaJoie's Seafood Orzo Salad

1 **cup uncooked orzo (rice-shaped pasta)**

2 **tablespoons olive oil, divided**

1/2 **pound medium shrimp, peeled and deveined**

1/2 **pound bay scallops**

1 **clove garlic, minced**

2 **green onions, sliced**

2 **tablespoons chopped fresh dill**

1 **tablespoon lemon juice**

1 **teaspoon salt**

1 **teaspoon TABASCO® brand Pepper Sauce**

Cook orzo according to package directions; drain. Meanwhile, heat 1 tablespoon of olive oil in a 12-inch skillet over medium-high heat. Add shrimp, scallops, and garlic and cook 5 minutes or until shrimp turns pink and scallops are opaque, stirring occasionally. In a large bowl, combine seafood, orzo, green onions, dill, lemon juice, salt, TABASCO® Sauce, and remaining 1 tablespoon olive oil; mix well. Serve immediately, or refrigerate and serve cold. Makes 4 servings.

Like father, like son! Randy LaJoie's dad started him in go-carts as a youngster. After years of hard work, Randy realized his racing dream in 1996 by winning the NASCAR Busch Series title. A year later, he became the first driver in 10 years to win the championship in two consecutive years.

Randy invites you to cook up a storm with his Seafood Orzo Salad.

Deb Williams' New Potato Salad

- 6 medium-size new red potatoes, cubed
- ⅓ cup olive or vegetable oil
- ¼ cup cider vinegar
- 1 tablespoon country-style Dijon mustard
- 1 small onion, chopped
- 1 clove garlic, minced
- 2 teaspoons TABASCO® brand Green Pepper Sauce
- ½ teaspoon salt
- 1 tablespoon chopped fresh dill, or ½ teaspoon dried
- 1 tablespoon chopped fresh tarragon, or ½ teaspoon dried

Cook potatoes in boiling water 10 to 15 minutes or until just tender; drain. In a large bowl, combine oil, vinegar, mustard, onion, garlic, TABASCO® Sauce, salt, dill, and tarragon; blend well. Add warm potatoes and toss to coat well. Cover and refrigerate at least 2 hours to blend flavors. Makes 6 servings.

Deb Williams covers the NASCAR Winston Cup Series for one of the largest racing publications in the country, *NASCAR Winston Cup Scene*. It's her dream come true to talk with drivers and crews, and then actually get to write about it!

Off the circuit, you'll find Deb perfecting her needlepoint, watching almost every football game, and serving her magnificent New Potato Salad.

Ted Musgrave's Spiced Wild Rice Mushroom Soup

²/₃ cup uncooked wild rice

4 cups water

1 (2½-ounce) package slivered almonds (about ½ cup)

¼ cup butter or margarine

8 ounces fresh mushrooms, sliced

1 stalk celery, thinly sliced

⅓ cup all-purpose flour

3 (10½-ounce) cans chicken broth

½ teaspoon curry powder

½ teaspoon dry mustard

1 teaspoon Worcestershire sauce

¼ to ½ teaspoon ground cinnamon

¼ teaspoon black pepper

1 teaspoon TABASCO® brand Pepper Sauce

2 cups half-and-half

Paprika

In a large saucepan over high heat, combine wild rice and water; bring to a boil. Reduce heat, cover, and simmer 30 minutes, stirring occasionally. Turn off heat and let sit 25 minutes longer. Drain and set aside.

In a small skillet over low heat, cook and stir almonds until lightly toasted; set aside. Melt butter in a large Dutch oven over medium heat; add mushrooms and celery and cook 2 minutes. Sprinkle flour over mixture; cook and stir 1 minute. Gradually add chicken broth, cooking and stirring until mixture is somewhat thickened. Stir in curry powder, mustard, Worcestershire sauce, cinnamon, pepper, TABASCO® Sauce, and half-and-half. Heat through. Ladle into bowls and sprinkle each serving with almonds and paprika. Makes 8 servings.

If Ted Musgrave seems both determined and modest, that's because he is. Moving into NASCAR Winston Cup competition in 1990, Musgrave was runner-up for Rookie of the Year honors.

Ted spends his free time restoring vintage cars and with his wife, Debbie, and family Brittany, Justin, and Ted Jr., stirring up this Spiced Wild Rice Mushroom Soup.

Greg Sacks' Scallop Stew

- 1/4 cup butter or margarine
- 2 tablespoons thinly sliced green onion tops
- 2 tablespoons all-purpose flour
- 2 cups half-and-half or whole milk
- 1/2 cup water
- 1 teaspoon TABASCO® brand Pepper Sauce
- 1/4 teaspoon salt
- 1/4 teaspoon black pepper
- 1 pint bay scallops
- 1 tablespoon chopped fresh parsley

Melt butter in a 3-quart saucepan over medium heat. Add green onion and cook 5 minutes, stirring often. Add flour and cook 1 minute, stirring constantly. Stir in half-and-half; cook and stir until smooth and thickened. Add water, TABASCO® Sauce, salt, and pepper and continue cooking and stirring until sauce is smooth and boiling. Add scallops and parsley and reduce heat to low. Cook 8 to 10 minutes longer or until scallops are opaque, stirring often; do not boil. Makes 4 servings.

Greg Sacks captured his first NASCAR Winston Cup win in the Firecracker 400 at Daytona in 1985 and in 1996 he earned his first career NASCAR Busch Series victory at Talladega.

Greg resides in New Smyrna Beach, Florida, where he and his family enjoy getting a gang together for a hearty Scallop Stew.

READY TO ROAR

It's "one-to-go" and the pack pulls in tight together. The pace car ducks off, the green flag waves, and the thunder rolls.

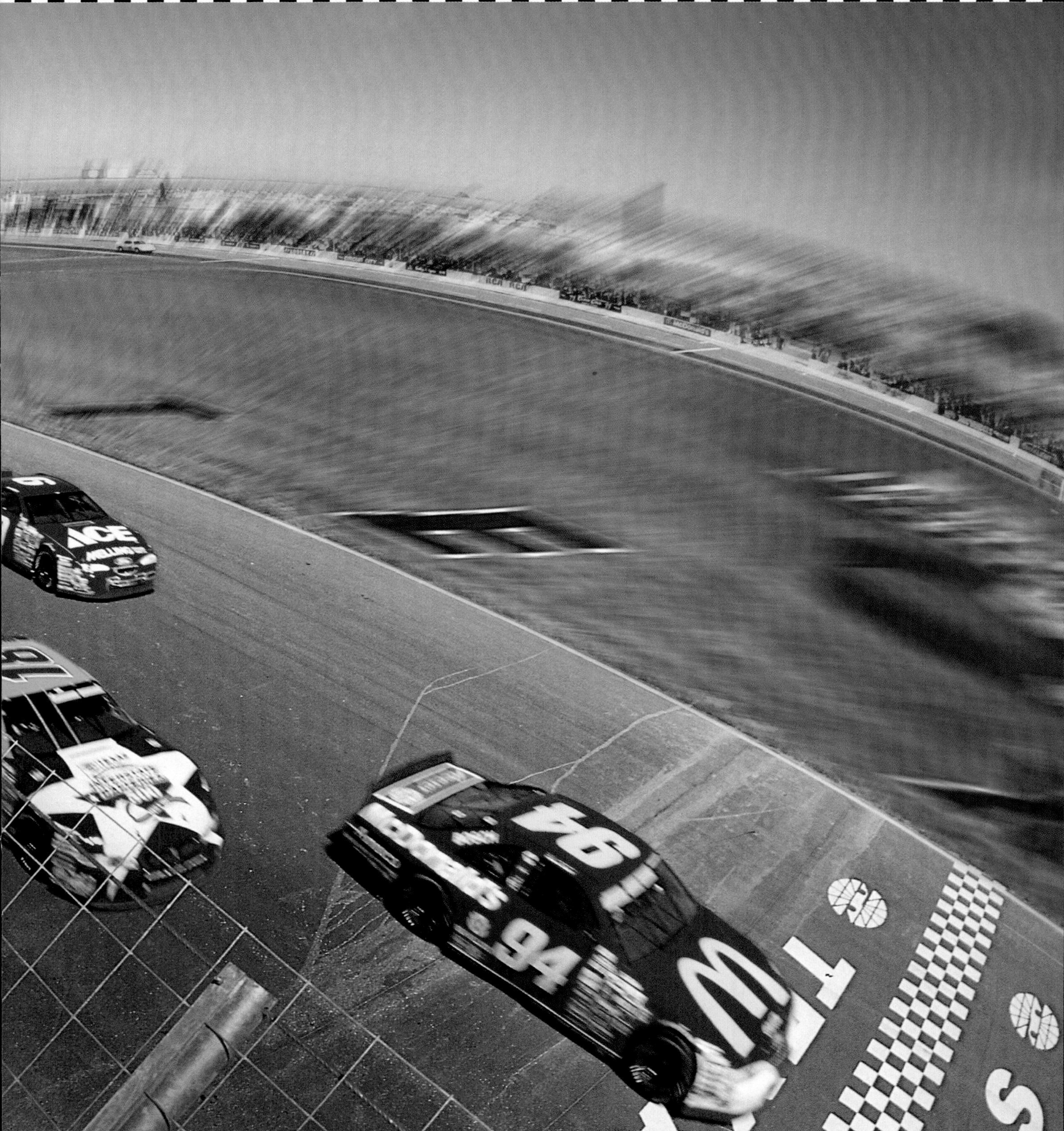
ACE
94

Todd Bodine's Roast Duck with Cumberland Sauce

1 (4-pound) duck

1 teaspoon TABASCO® brand Pepper Sauce, divided

Salt

3/4 cup currant jelly

3/4 cup orange juice

1/4 cup lemon juice

1/4 teaspoon ground ginger

1 tablespoon cornstarch

2 tablespoons water

Preheat oven to 375°F. Pierce skin of duck with a fork. Rub duck with 1/2 teaspoon of TABASCO® Sauce and sprinkle with salt. Place on a rack in a roasting pan and roast 1 1/2 hours or until temperature of meat reaches 190°F. Meanwhile prepare Cumberland Sauce: Melt jelly in a small saucepan over medium heat; stir in orange and lemon juices, ginger, and remaining 1/2 teaspoon TABASCO® Sauce. In a small bowl dissolve cornstarch in water; stir in to jelly mixture. Bring to a boil, stirring constantly, and boil 1 minute. Serve sauce with roast duck. Makes 4 servings.

No one exemplifies both the past and the future of NASCAR racing more than Todd Bodine. The youngest of three racing brothers, Todd continues a legacy started by his father and grandfather. Born in Chemung, New York, he spent his early years around the family track doing everything you'd expect a young kid looking for a break to do, including working in the pits and changing tires.

Todd's dedication, at 33, is as fierce as the competition, and that includes his two best competitors—his brothers Brett and Geoff. "I've been very lucky," Todd says. "Racing was in my blood."

Today, Todd is the proud driver of TEAM TABASCO®—the latest entry into the NASCAR Winston Cup Series. Todd, his wife, Lynn, and his entire crew are excited to command a car that's sure to add fire and sizzle to NASCAR competition…and to introduce their Roast Duck with Cumberland Sauce.

John Graham's Cornish Hens with Oyster Dressing

- ³/₄ cup butter or margarine, divided
- 1 cup chopped onion
- 1 cup chopped celery
- ¹/₂ cup chopped shallots
- ¹/₂ cup chopped red bell pepper
- ¹/₂ cup chopped green bell pepper
- 2 cloves garlic, minced
- 2 bay leaves
- 2 dozen shucked oysters with liquid
- ³/₄ teaspoon dried thyme leaves, crumbled and divided
- ¹/₂ teaspoon dried oregano leaves, crumbled
- ³/₄ teaspoon TABASCO® brand Pepper Sauce, divided
- 5 cups cooked rice
- 6 Cornish game hens
- ¹/₄ teaspoon salt
- 1 tablespoon all-purpose flour
- 1 cup chicken broth

Melt ¹/₂ cup of butter in a large skillet over medium heat; add onion, celery, shallots, bell peppers, garlic, and bay leaves and cook 5 minutes. Coarsely chop oysters, reserving liquid. Stir oysters into skillet with ¹/₂ teaspoon of thyme, oregano, and ¹/₂ teaspoon of TABASCO® Sauce; simmer 5 minutes longer. Remove bay leaves. Stir in rice and oyster liquid, mixing well.

Preheat oven to 350°F. Wash Cornish hens and pat dry; stuff cavities with rice stuffing. Place remaining stuffing in a greased baking dish and cover. Arrange hens on a rack in a shallow roasting pan. Melt remaining ¹/₄ cup butter; stir in salt and remaining ¹/₄ teaspoon thyme and ¹/₄ teaspoon TABASCO® Sauce. Brush hens with butter mixture and bake, uncovered, for 1¹/₂ hours or until tender, basting often with pan drippings. During last half hour, bake extra stuffing in covered dish. Spoon extra stuffing onto a platter and arrange hens on top; keep warm.

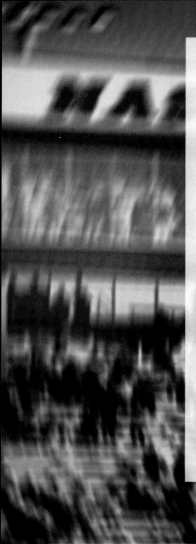

John Graham is right in the middle of it all! He's the president of Daytona International Speedway and proudly oversees the track that hosts the most prestigious event on the NASCAR Winston Cup Series—the Daytona 500—which also opens the circuit's racing season.

John takes the challenge all in stride, running a facility that's so large, it

To make gravy, pour excess fat from roasting pan and discard; add flour to pan and stir until well blended. Place pan on stove top over medium heat; gradually add broth and scrape bits from bottom of pan, stirring constantly until mixture thickens and boils. Serve with hens. Makes 6 servings.

has a 44-acre lake in the middle. For pure relaxation, John kicks back and enjoys the competition of computer games—"always being a kid at heart and never, ever growing up!"

Wherever there are drivers, crews, and fans, you'll find John, most likely serving up his famous Cornish Hens with Oyster Dressing.

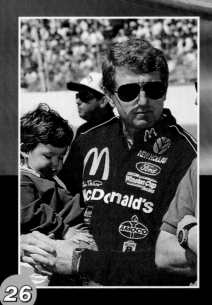

NASCAR is a family sport! Just take a look at the talented Elliott brothers—Ernie, Dan, and, of course, "Million Dollar Bill."

After more than 20 years on the NASCAR Winston Cup circuit, Bill Elliott is more determined than ever to expand on his 40 career wins, 48 career pole positions, and, one of his proudest career achievements, being

Bill Elliott's Snappy Pea and Chicken Pot Pie

- 3   **cups chicken broth**
- 2   **skinless, boneless chicken breast halves, cut into 1-inch chunks**
- 1   **medium baking potato, peeled and cut into $1/2$-inch cubes**
- $1^1/_2$ **cups carrots cut into $1/2$-inch slices**
- 1   **cup frozen pearl onions**
- 1   **teaspoon TABASCO® brand Pepper Sauce**
- $1/_2$ **teaspoon dried rosemary**
- 1   **red bell pepper, coarsely chopped**
- 4   **ounces sugar snap peas, halved lengthwise (about 1 cup)**
- 3   **tablespoons butter or margarine**
- $1/_4$ **cup all-purpose flour**
- 1   **egg, beaten**
- $1/_2$ **(17.25-ounce) box frozen puff pastry (1 sheet)**

In a large heavy saucepan, bring chicken broth to a boil; add chicken and return to a boil. Stir in potato, carrots, onions, TABASCO® Sauce, rosemary, and *$1/_4$ teaspoon salt*. Reduce heat to medium-low; cover and simmer 8 to 10 minutes or until vegetables are tender. Add bell pepper and peas; boil 30 seconds or just until peas turn bright green. Drain mixture through a colander suspended over a bowl to catch chicken broth; set aside.

Melt butter in a medium saucepan over low heat. Stir in flour and cook 3 to 4 minutes, stirring constantly. Pour in 2 cups of reserved chicken broth and whisk until smooth. Bring to a boil, stirring constantly. Reduce heat to low and simmer 5 minutes or until thickened and bubbly, stirring frequently; set aside.

Preheat oven to 425°F. Defrost pastry according to package directions and unfold on floured surface. Meanwhile, spoon chicken mixture into a lightly buttered shallow $1^1/_2$-quart baking dish; spoon sauce on top. Combine beaten egg and *1 teaspoon water* and brush onto outside rim of baking dish. Place pastry over dish and press firmly around edge to seal; trim dough to make neat edge. Brush top with egg mixture. Place dish on a baking sheet and bake 15 minutes or until pastry is puffed and golden brown. Serve at once. Makes 4 servings.

voted the most popular driver on the tour by his fans a record 12 times!

What does Bill like to do off the track? How about seeking more excitement! He's both an avid skier and a pilot, often flying himself to the racetracks or choice locations around the country to ski.

Fans call him "Awesome Bill from Dawsonville." Awesome is his Snappy Pea and Chicken Pot Pie, something any Georgia native would be proud of.

Grant Lynch's Venison Ragoût with Parsley Biscuits

- 1/4 pound bacon, diced
- 1 pound boneless venison shoulder, cut into 1-inch chunks
- 3 large carrots, peeled and cut into 1/2-inch slices
- 3 large parsnips, peeled and cut into 1/2-inch slices
- 1 cup fresh or frozen pearl onions
- 1 tablespoon butter or margarine
- 6 ounces mushrooms, cut in half
- 2 cloves garlic, minced
- 1 cup red wine
- 1 tablespoon cornstarch
- 1 cup water
- 2 tablespoons chopped fresh parsley
- 1 tablespoon tomato paste
- 1 teaspoon salt
- 1 teaspoon TABASCO® brand Pepper Sauce
- 1/2 teaspoon dried thyme leaves, crumbled

Parsley Biscuits

- 2 cups all-purpose flour
- 1 tablespoon baking powder
- 1/2 teaspoon baking soda
- 1/2 teaspoon salt
- 1/4 cup butter or margarine, cut into small pieces
- 1 cup buttermilk
- 3 tablespoons chopped fresh parsley

In a 12-inch skillet over medium heat, cook bacon just until crisp, stirring occasionally. With a slotted spoon, remove from skillet to a bowl. Add venison to drippings in skillet and cook over medium-high heat until well browned on all sides, stirring frequently; remove to bowl with bacon. Add carrots, parsnips, and onions to drippings in skillet and cook 5 minutes over medium heat. Add butter, mushrooms, and garlic; cook 5 minutes longer or until vegetables are crisp-tender, stirring occasionally.

Preheat oven to 350°F. Combine wine and cornstarch in a small bowl and stir until blended; add to skillet along with water, parsley, tomato paste, salt, TABASCO® Sauce, thyme, cooked bacon, and venison. Bring to a boil. Spoon mixture into 2-quart shallow casserole; cover with foil and bake for 30 minutes. Meanwhile, prepare Parsley Biscuit batter: Combine flour, baking powder, baking soda, and salt in a medium bowl; mix well. Cut butter into flour mixture with a

Grant Lynch first realized his passion for racing behind the wheel, driving show cars across the country for NASCAR Winston Cup Series' sponsor R.J. Reynolds. In 1982, he simply drove to the nearest track, and he's been around racing ever since.

There's a very special talent in managing a team, and Grant has worked his way up to become the president of Talladega Superspeedway, the largest track in NASCAR racing.

pastry blender until mixture resembles coarse crumbs. Add buttermilk and parsley and stir just until moistened.

Remove casserole from oven; increase oven temperature to 450°F. Carefully uncover casserole. Using a ⅓-cup measure, drop biscuit batter onto ragoût in casserole to make 6 biscuits. Bake, uncovered, for 12 to 15 minutes or until biscuits are golden. Makes 6 servings.

In the heart of Alabama, Talladega Superspeedway hosts more than 150,000 NASCAR fans two Sundays a year. He enjoys the memories and spirit that arrive with every race and the distinguished bond between the drivers and their fans.

He's an avid hunter away from the track, so be sure to try his special Venison Ragoût with Parsley Biscuits.

Dave Marcis' Three-Pepper Sausage Sauté

1   pound hot Italian sausage

1   large red bell pepper

1   large green bell pepper

1   large yellow bell pepper

1   medium onion

1   teaspoon dried oregano leaves, crumbled

2   teaspoons TABASCO® brand Green Pepper Sauce

1/2 teaspoon salt

1/4 cup water

In a large skillet over medium heat, cook sausage 15 minutes or until browned on all sides, turning occasionally and pricking with a fork. Meanwhile, cut peppers into 1/2-inch slices; cut onion in half and cut each half into 1/2-inch slices.

Remove sausage to a cutting board. In drippings remaining in skillet, cook peppers and onion about 5 minutes, stirring occasionally. When sausages cool enough to handle, cut into 1-inch slices and add to skillet. Stir in oregano, TABASCO® Sauce, salt, and water. Bring to a boil; reduce heat to low, cover, and simmer 5 minutes to blend flavors. Makes 4 servings.

Dave Marcis first put the "pedal to the metal" back in Wausau, Wisconsin, more than 30 years ago and as far as we know never plans to stop! Dave is the owner and driver of his racing team and is now in his third decade on the tour.
What gets him away from his passion? Hunting, fishing, and snowmobiling! And often, this hearty Three-Pepper Sausage Sauté.

Michael Waltrip's Pork Chops with Apples and Bourbon

- 4 (1-inch-thick) boneless pork loin chops, trimmed of fat
- 1 clove garlic, halved lengthwise

Pinch of dried sage leaves, crumbled

- 2 tablespoons unsalted butter or margarine
- 1/2 teaspoon TABASCO® brand Pepper Sauce
- 1 teaspoon lemon juice
- 1/2 cup chopped onion
- 1 medium cooking apple, unpeeled and sliced
- 1/3 cup bourbon or apple cider

Pat pork chops dry; rub each on both sides with cut sides of garlic and sprinkle with sage. Melt butter in a large skillet over medium-high heat; add TABASCO® Sauce and, when butter sizzles, add pork chops. Cook 12 to 14 minutes, turning once, or until chops are golden brown on both sides and cooked through. Remove from pan, sprinkle with lemon juice, and keep warm. Add onion to skillet and cook over medium heat for 1 minute; stir in apple and cook 1 minute. Add bourbon and cook 1 minute longer, stirring often. Spoon sauce over pork chops and serve. Makes 4 servings.

Before racing in the NASCAR Winston Cup Series, Michael Waltrip won the NASCAR Goody's Dash Series title in 1983 and was voted the series' most popular driver that year and also in '84.

He's his brother Darrell's biggest fan, but has made a career of his own, proving there's no substitute for skill and determination. There's no substitute for his Pork Chops with Apples and Bourbon either!

Mike Helton's Chicken, Pork, and Sausage Jambalaya

- 4 tablespoons vegetable oil, divided
- 3 pounds cut-up chicken pieces
- 1/2 pound boneless pork, cut into thin strips
- 1/2 pound andouille or smoked sausage, cut into 1/2-inch slices
- 1 cup sliced celery
- 1 cup chopped onion
- 1 cup chopped green bell pepper
- 1 clove garlic, minced
- 2 (14.5-ounce) cans diced tomatoes, undrained
- 1 cup chicken broth
- 1 (6-ounce) can tomato paste
- 1 tablespoon TABASCO® brand Green Pepper Sauce
- 1 bay leaf
- 1/2 teaspoon salt
- 1 teaspoon dried oregano leaves, crumbled
- 1 teaspoon dried thyme leaves, crumbled
- 1/2 teaspoon ground allspice
- 1/2 cup uncooked rice

Heat 2 tablespoons of oil in a heavy 5-quart Dutch oven over medium-high heat. Add chicken and brown on all sides, about 10 minutes; remove chicken. Heat remaining 2 tablespoons oil in Dutch oven and add pork, sausage, celery, onion, green pepper, and garlic; cook 8 to 10 minutes or until tender, stirring often. Stir in tomatoes, chicken broth, tomato paste, TABASCO® Sauce, bay leaf, salt, oregano, thyme, and allspice; mix well. Return chicken to pot; cover, reduce heat to low, and simmer 10 minutes. Stir in rice. Cover and simmer 40 minutes or until rice is tender, stirring frequently and adding additional broth if rice begins to stick to bottom of pot. Makes 8 servings.

As vice-president for competition for NASCAR, Mike Helton has to wear a lot of different hats. From working with drivers, teams, and tracks on the week-to-week operations of running the NASCAR Winston Cup and NASCAR Busch Series to dealing with television networks covering each event, Helton's plate stays plenty full.

When Mike, who is the former president of Talladega Superspeedway, isn't working on keeping the competition hot on the racetrack, he's keeping his friend's plates full with his extra-zesty Chicken, Pork, and Sausage Jambalaya.

Jeff Burton's Peach-Glazed Virginia Ham

Glazed Ham:

1 (8-pound) smoked Virginia ham (shank end)

$1/2$ cup peach preserves

1 tablespoon coarse-grained mustard

$3/4$ teaspoon TABASCO® brand Pepper Sauce

$1/8$ teaspoon ground cloves

Peach-Corn Piccalilli:

3 large ripe peaches

1 tablespoon vegetable oil

1 medium red bell pepper, diced

$1/4$ cup sliced green onion

1 (17-ounce) can whole kernel corn, drained

2 tablespoons brown sugar

2 tablespoons cider vinegar

1 teaspoon TABASCO® brand Pepper Sauce

$1/4$ teaspoon salt

Preheat oven to 325°F. Remove skin from ham; trim off excess fat, leaving a thin layer. Score fat $1/4$-inch deep in a 1-inch diamond pattern. Place ham, fat side up, in roasting pan; insert meat thermometer into thickest part of ham, so tip is not touching bone. Bake, uncovered, about $1^1/2$ hours or until thermometer reaches 135°F. Meanwhile, make glaze: In a small bowl, combine peach preserves, mustard, TABASCO® Sauce, and cloves. Remove ham from oven and brush with peach glaze. Bake 20 minutes longer or until temperature reaches 140°F.

Jeff's older brother Ward got him started steering go-carts. It wasn't long before Jeff switched to open stocks on the short tracks in his hometown of South Boston, Virginia, where he was proudly named South Boston's Most Popular Driver in 1988.

Focused and fearless, Jeff made his NASCAR Winston Cup debut in 1993

Prepare Peach-Corn Piccalilli: Cut peaches in half and remove pits; chop 2 halves and set aside. Heat oil in a 2-quart saucepan over medium heat. Add bell pepper and green onion; cook 3 minutes, stirring frequently. Add corn, brown sugar, vinegar, TABASCO® Sauce, and salt; mix well and bring to a boil. Stir in chopped peaches; reduce heat to low, cover, and simmer 5 minutes or just until peaches are tender.

To serve, arrange ham on a large platter. Fill peach halves with piccalilli and arrange around ham; serve additional piccalilli on the side. Makes 8 to 12 servings.

and a year later was named the NASCAR Winston Cup Rookie of the Year. He won his first NASCAR Winston Cup race in April of 1997 and won twice more before the year was over. A man on the move, Jeff's determined to make Victory Lane a regular stop.

Between boating and his passion for rock'n'roll, you'll find him turning up the heat with his favorite recipe. Naturally, it's Peach-Glazed Virginia Ham.

Dale Earnhardt's Fish and Vegetable Rolls

12 asparagus spears

2 carrots, peeled and cut into thin strips

¹/₄ cup mayonnaise

2 tablespoons seasoned dry bread crumbs

2 tablespoons country-style Dijon mustard

1 tablespoon chopped fresh dill or 1 teaspoon dried

1 teaspoon TABASCO® brand Pepper Sauce

4 flounder or sole fillets

In a 12-inch skillet over high heat, combine asparagus, carrots, and enough water to cover vegetables; bring to a boil. Reduce heat to low and simmer 2 to 3 minutes or until vegetables are crisp-tender; drain. Preheat oven to 450°F. In a small bowl, combine mayonnaise, bread crumbs, mustard, dill, and TABASCO® Sauce. Spread half of mixture on top sides of fish fillets. Top each fillet with one-fourth of cooked asparagus and carrots. Roll fish around vegetables and place seam side down in a greased 12x8x2-inch baking dish. Spread remaining mustard mixture on tops of fish rolls. Bake 12 to 15 minutes or until fish flakes easily when tested with a fork. Makes 4 servings.

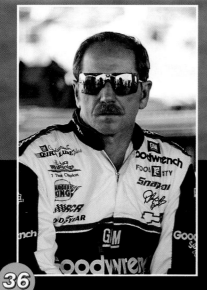

Dale Earnhardt was born in North Carolina, the heart of racing country, so it should come as no surprise that he was born to race—and win! How about 70 NASCAR Winston Cup wins and a record-tying (with Richard Petty) seven series championships.

What does it take to rack up those kinds of numbers? Dedication, a

burning desire to win, the ability to intimidate the competition, and the ability to take things in stride.

"You win some, you lose some," says Earnhardt matter-of-factly. But if that's the true grit it takes, then Dale's got it, almost single-handedly dominating the circuit for the past decade.

Dale still lives in North Carolina with his wife Teresa and family—cooking up a storm with Fish and Vegetable Rolls.

Terry Labonte's Catfish with Tomato-Jalapeño Chutney

4¹/₂ cups KELLOGG'S CORN FLAKES® cereal, crushed to 2 cups

³/₄ cup milk

1 egg, beaten

¹/₄ teaspoon salt

4 fillets farm-raised catfish (1 to 1¹/₂ pounds)

Vegetable cooking spray

1 tablespoon vegetable oil

¹/₂ cup finely chopped onion

¹/₂ cup finely chopped green bell pepper

¹/₄ cup finely chopped celery

1 clove garlic, minced

³/₄ cup water

1 (6-ounce) can tomato paste

2 tablespoons TABASCO® brand Green Pepper Sauce

Preheat oven to 350°F. Place crushed corn flakes in a shallow dish or pan. In another shallow dish, combine milk, egg, and salt; stir until mixed well. Dip fish into egg mixture, then coat with crushed corn flakes. Place on a greased baking sheet and spray fish lightly with vegetable cooking spray. Bake 25 to 30 minutes or until fish flakes easily when tested with a fork.

Meanwhile, prepare Tomato-Jalapeño Chutney: Heat oil in a saucepan over medium heat; stir in onion, bell pepper, celery, and garlic and cook 5 minutes or until tender, stirring often. Add water, tomato paste, and TABASCO® Sauce and mix well. Simmer 8 to 10 minutes longer, stirring often. Serve with catfish. Makes 4 servings.

Consistency and respect. Those are two words that describe Terry Labonte's racing career since he first hit the track more than 20 years ago. They're certainly well-earned accolades, since the "Iron Man" has started more NASCAR Winston Cup races in a row (560-plus and counting), winning two series championships and finishing in the top five more than 175 times in the process.

The "Ice Man"—as solid and trusted as any hero in NASCAR history—Terry's out to continue to keep the respect and loyalty of both his competitors and his fans.

A native of Corpus Christi, Texas, Terry—with his wife, Kim, and their kids, Kristi and Justin—enjoys the North Carolina countryside, where he often grills his big catch, Catfish with Tomato-Jalapeño Chutney.

Ned Jarrett's Shrimp and Crab Casserole

- 1/8 cup all-purpose flour
- 1/4 teaspoon black pepper
- 2 cups milk, divided
- 1/3 cup pasteurized processed cheese sauce
- 1/2 teaspoon TABASCO® brand Pepper Sauce
- 1/2 pound medium shrimp, cooked, peeled, and deveined (about 1 1/4 cups)
- 1/4 pound crabmeat (about 3/4 cup)
- 1 cup shredded cheddar cheese

Hot cooked rice (optional)

Preheat oven to 350°F. In a small bowl, combine flour, pepper, and 1/4 cup of milk; beat with a whisk or fork until smooth and set aside. Pour remaining milk into top of double boiler and place over simmering water on medium-high heat; add cheese sauce and heat until melted. Stir in TABASCO® Sauce and flour mixture; cook and stir until smooth and thickened, about 5 minutes. Remove from heat and gently stir in shrimp and crabmeat. Pour into a shallow 2-quart baking dish and sprinkle cheese on top. Bake 15 to 20 minutes or until cheese is melted. Serve over rice, if desired. Makes 6 to 8 servings.

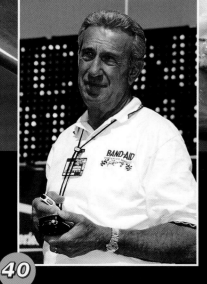

Ned Jarrett's got 50 NASCAR Winston Cup victories and two championships—truly making him a legend. What did he do for an encore when he retired? He became one of NASCAR's most beloved sportscasters!

Off season, you'll find Ned casting for trout. So to no one's surprise, his favorite meal is seafood—especially this Shrimp and Crab Casserole.

Benny Parsons' Captain's Crabmeat

- 1/4 cup butter or margarine
- 1/2 pound mushrooms, thinly sliced
- 1 small green bell pepper, cut into julienne strips
- 1/2 cup diced celery
- 1/2 cup thinly sliced green onion
- 2 (10 3/4-ounce) cans condensed cream of celery soup, undiluted
- 1/4 cup lemon juice
- 1 (2-ounce) jar chopped pimento
- 1/4 cup sliced black olives
- 2 tablespoons chopped fresh parsley
- 1 teaspoon TABASCO® brand Pepper Sauce
- 12 ounces fresh or frozen crabmeat (about 2 1/2 cups)
- 6 frozen patty shells, baked according to package directions, or hot cooked rice
- 1/2 cup slivered almonds, toasted

Melt butter in a large skillet over medium heat. Add mushrooms, bell pepper, celery, and green onion; cook and stir until vegetables are tender, about 5 minutes. Stir in condensed soup, lemon juice, pimento, olives, parsley, and TABASCO® Sauce; mix well and heat through, stirring often. Meanwhile, pick through crabmeat to remove any shell or cartilage; add crabmeat to skillet and heat through. Serve over patty shells or rice; sprinkle almonds on top. Makes 6 servings.

Benny Parsons was the first driver to post an official qualifying speed faster than 200 mph (in 1982) for a NASCAR Winston Cup event. In addition to 21 career wins, he also won the 1973 NASCAR Winston Cup championship.

Today, you'll find Benny talking it up for ESPN and ABC as well as hosting a weekly radio show or at home cooking up some of his Captain's Crabmeat.

TRADING PAINT

Precision handling enables you to "brush up" against a competitor and pass. Winning makes it a risk worth taking.

Eli Gold's Barbecued Shrimp

"We like real spicy food, especially Cajun food," says Eli, who travels to south Louisiana often to broadcast at sports events. Barbecued shrimp originated in New Orleans, but actually it is not barbecued at all.

- 1 **cup butter or margarine**
- 1/2 **cup olive oil**
- 1/4 **cup minced garlic (8 to 10 large cloves)**
- 1/4 **cup cracked black pepper**
- 1/4 **cup Worcestershire sauce**
- 2 **tablespoons dried basil leaves, crumbled**
- 1 **tablespoon dried thyme leaves, crumbled**
- 1 to 2 **tablespoons TABASCO® brand Pepper Sauce**
- 3 **pounds large shrimp (21 to 25 count), preferably with heads on**

Hot French bread

Preheat oven to 375°F. Heat butter and olive oil in a saucepan over medium heat until butter is melted. Add garlic, pepper, Worcestershire sauce, basil, thyme, and TABASCO® Sauce. Cook and stir 1 to 2 minutes and remove from heat. Place shrimp in an 18x13x1-inch baking pan and pour butter mixture on top; toss to coat and arrange shrimp evenly in pan. Bake 8 minutes, then stir shrimp to coat with butter mixture again. Bake 6 to 8 minutes longer or until shrimp turn pink and are cooked through; do not overcook. Serve in bowls, using French bread to dip in sauce. Makes 6 servings.

Is there anything more exciting than racing in the Daytona 500? Eli Gold thinks so—it's broadcasting the Daytona 500 to millions of radio listeners. For 20 years he's been a NASCAR commentator and announcer on the Motor Racing Network (MRN).

The unique advantage Eli has is that he truly gets "up close and personal"

with the supercharged action of each event and gets to know the drivers and their teams. It adds up to some of racing's most colorful commentary.

Like his broadcasts, his grilling runs hot and fiery. Give him some of his Barbecued Shrimp, and you've topped off his day—just as it will yours.

Geoff Bodine's Hot Grilled Trout

- ¹/₄ cup lemon juice
- 2 tablespoons melted butter or margarine
- 2 tablespoons vegetable oil
- 2 tablespoons chopped fresh parsley
- 2 tablespoons sesame seeds
- 1 tablespoon TABASCO® brand Pepper Sauce
- ¹/₂ teaspoon ground ginger
- ¹/₂ teaspoon salt
- 4 (1-pound) brook trout, cleaned

In a shallow dish, combine lemon juice, butter, oil, parsley, sesame seeds, TABASCO® Sauce, ginger, and salt; mix well. Pierce skin of fish in several places with a fork. Roll fish in lemon juice mixture to coat inside and out. Leave fish in marinade, cover dish, and refrigerate 30 minutes to 1 hour, turning fish occasionally. Meanwhile, preheat grill. Remove fish from marinade, reserving marinade. Place fish in a handheld grill basket; brush fish with reserved marinade. Place on grill about 4 inches above heat and cook 5 minutes. Turn, brush with marinade again, and cook 5 minutes longer or until fish flakes easily when tested with fork. Serve with additional TABASCO® Sauce, if desired. Makes 4 servings.

Geoff Bodine got his start in NASCAR modified racing, which gave him the edge to swiftly cruise into NASCAR Winston Cup Series competition. He has since won the Daytona 500 plus 17 others.

He's doesn't mince words, and he's not afraid to trade paint with anyone, in any race. But true to the generosity and compassion in NASCAR racing,

Geoff donated his Busch Pole Award bonus in 1994 to Ernie Irvan's favorite charity after the accident that forced Irvan to miss the final portion of that season. That's what sets the NASCAR family apart from all the rest.

Geoff would also like to share, with you, his favorite recipe for Hot Grilled Trout.

Ricky Rudd's Spicy Crab Cakes with Jalapeño Tartar Sauce

- 2   cups fresh or frozen crabmeat, flaked (about 1/2 pound)
- 3/4 cup fine dry bread crumbs
- 1/4 cup finely chopped onion
- 1   egg
- 1   teaspoon TABASCO® brand Pepper Sauce
- 1/2 teaspoon salt
- 2   tablespoons butter or margarine
- 1/2 cup mayonnaise
- 1   tablespoon chopped sweet pickle
- 2   teaspoons TABASCO® brand Green Pepper Sauce

Pick through crabmeat to remove any shell or cartilage. In a large bowl, combine crabmeat, bread crumbs, onion, egg, TABASCO® Pepper Sauce, and salt; mix well and shape into four 3-inch patties. Melt butter in a 12-inch skillet over medium heat; add patties and cook 5 minutes on each side or until golden brown. Meanwhile, prepare Jalapeño Tartar Sauce: In a small bowl, combine mayonnaise, pickle, and TABASCO® Green Pepper Sauce; mix well and serve with crab cakes. Makes 4 servings.

At 21, Ricky Rudd was named the NASCAR Winston Cup Series Rookie of the Year. Today, he has a long stretch of consecutive winning seasons—15 ! Both a driver and a car owner, he's considered one of the foremost racers on the circuit.

At home, Ricky, his wife Linda, and son Landon, stir up lots of action with their Spicy Crab Cakes with Jalapeño Tartar Sauce.

Jane Hogan's
Fire and Ice Salad

4   (6-ounce) fillets fish or chicken

Lemon pepper seasoning to taste

Baby greens, romaine, or butterhead
lettuce, torn into bite-size pieces

1   medium red onion, sliced into
    thin rings

1   green bell pepper, diced

1   pint fresh strawberries, sliced

1   (16-ounce) can unsweetened
    pineapple chunks, drained

1/2 cup safflower oil

1/2 cup seasoned rice vinegar

2   tablespoons TABASCO® brand
    Green Pepper Sauce

4   tablespoons chopped fresh cilantro

Preheat grill or broiler. Season
fillets with lemon pepper and grill
or broil 4 to 6 inches from heat
for about 4 minutes per side or
until done; cool and cut into bite-
size pieces. Arrange greens on
four plates; top with fish or
chicken, onion, bell pepper,
strawberries, and pineapple. In a
cruet or bottle, combine oil,
vinegar, and TABASCO® Sauce;
shake well. Drizzle dressing over
salads and sprinkle on cilantro.
Makes 4 servings.

Jane Hogan has been cooking food for drivers and fans since 1965. She
travels to almost every NASCAR Winston Cup Series event, bringing her famous pepper jelly. She bakes cherry pies for Rusty Wallace and apple pies for Dale Earnhardt
and brings a batch of chocolate chip cookies for Jeff Gordon and his crew.
Jane thinks this Fire and Ice Salad will soon become quite a tradition itself.

Darrell Waltrip's Hot Poulet

2 tablespoons TABASCO® brand Pepper Sauce

2 teaspoons ground cumin

2 teaspoons garlic powder

1½ teaspoons salt, divided

8 chicken thighs

1 tablespoon vegetable oil

1 medium onion, chopped

1 (10-ounce) package frozen cut okra, thawed

1 large tomato, chopped

2 tablespoons water

1 tablespoon TABASCO® brand Green Pepper Sauce

In a small bowl, combine TABASCO® Pepper Sauce, cumin, garlic powder, and 1 teaspoon of salt; mix well. Brush mixture on both sides of chicken and place in a bowl or pan to marinate; cover and refrigerate 4 to 6 hours or overnight. Preheat oven to 425°F. Place chicken in a shallow baking pan and bake 35 to 40 minutes or until chicken is no longer pink and skin is crisp and browned. Meanwhile, heat oil in a 10-inch nonreactive skillet over medium heat; add onion and cook until tender, about 5 minutes. Add okra, tomato, water, TABASCO® Green Pepper Sauce, and remaining ½ teaspoon salt. Bring to a boil, then reduce heat to low; cover and simmer 10 minutes or until okra is tender, stirring occasionally. Serve with chicken. Makes 4 servings.

In 1972, Darrell Waltrip ran his first NASCAR Winston Cup Series race. Twenty-six years, 3 NASCAR Winston Cup championships, and 84 victories later he's still a force to be reckoned with.

Darrell easily goes from behind the wheel to behind a grill, where he, wife Stevie, and daughters Jessica Leigh and Sarah share a mean Hot Poulet.

Harry Gant's
Grilled Spicy Steak

2   teaspoons TABASCO® brand Pepper Sauce

1   teaspoon salt

1/2   teaspoon garlic powder

1/2   teaspoon dried thyme leaves, crumbled

1/8   teaspoon ground allspice

1   (1-pound) boneless beef top sirloin steak

In a small bowl, combine TABASCO® Sauce, salt, garlic powder, thyme, and allspice and mix well; rub into both sides of steak. Cover and refrigerate at least 1 hour or overnight. Bring to room temperature before grilling. Preheat grill or broiler. Place steak on rack in grill or broiler pan; cook steak 8 minutes for medium-rare, or to desired doneness, turning once. Makes 2 servings.

In 1994, Harry Gant ended his NASCAR Winston Cup driving career with 18 wins and 474 starts. The next year he jumped into a pickup truck to race in the new NASCAR Craftsman Truck Series for one season. Now Harry builds houses and keeps up with his steakhouse in Taylorsville, North Carolina. At home he likes to toss this Grilled Spicy Steak on a sizzling BBQ grill.

Jim Hunter's Texas Chili

1/4 cup salad oil

3 pounds beef round or chuck, cut into 1-inch cubes

3 cloves garlic, minced

4 to 6 tablespoons chili powder

2 teaspoons salt

2 teaspoons dried oregano leaves, crumbled

2 teaspoons ground cumin

2 tablespoons TABASCO® brand Green Pepper Sauce

1 1/2 quarts water

1/3 cup white cornmeal

Heat oil in a large saucepan or Dutch oven over medium heat. Add beef and brown on all sides. Add garlic, chili powder, salt, oregano, cumin, TABASCO® Sauce, and water; mix well. Bring to a boil, cover, and reduce heat to low. Simmer 1 1/4 hours, stirring occasionally. Stir in cornmeal and mix well; simmer, uncovered, an additional 30 minutes or until meat is tender. If desired, serve with additional TABASCO® Sauce, chopped onion, rice, and beans. Makes 6 to 8 servings.

Jim Hunter covered NASCAR racing as a journalist for years. He later found himself working for NASCAR, where he eventually became the Vice President for Administration.

Jim now calls Darlington Raceway—a.k.a. the track "Too Tough to Tame"— his home, serving as its president and general manager. Every driver who's

ever earned his place on the charts has raced Darlington, the oldest track on the NASCAR Winston Cup circuit.

It's with pride that Jim's track is home to the NMPA Stock Car Hall of Fame and the famous Joe Weatherly Museum, which boasts a superb collection of remarkable racing and driver memorabilia.

However, nothing's more remarkable than his Texas Chili.

Steve Park's Spicy Pepper Penne

1/4 cup olive oil

3 red bell peppers, cut into 3x1/4-inch strips

2 large onions, diced

2 large cloves garlic, crushed

1 teaspoon salt

1 cup chicken broth

1 cup frozen peas

1 teaspoon TABASCO® brand Pepper Sauce

1/2 cup heavy cream or half-and-half

16 ounces penne pasta, cooked according to package directions

3/4 cup grated Parmesan or Romano cheese

Heat olive oil in a large skillet over medium heat. Add red peppers, onions, garlic, and salt; cook and stir 5 to 8 minutes or until vegetables are crisp-tender. Add chicken broth, peas, and TABASCO® Sauce and bring to a boil; reduce heat to low and cook, uncovered, for 5 minutes or until vegetables are tender, stirring occasionally.

Spoon half of red pepper mixture into container of food processor or blender; process until smooth and return to skillet over low heat. Stir in cream and heat through. Remove from heat and stir in pasta, tossing well; spoon into individual pasta bowls and top with cheese. Makes 6 servings.

No one can deny that the young Steve Park has already made an indelible mark on NASCAR racing. In 1997 he was named the NASCAR Busch Series Rookie of the Year and set more rookie records than any other first-year driver in series history—most wins, most top-five and top-ten finishes.
You could probably say Steve got the bug for racing from his father, who

still races modifieds in the Northeast. No matter where it came from, he has made it to the NASCAR Winston Cup Series where he will surely be a star.

Steve has a deep respect for the sport, his car and crew, and especially his many fans. That makes both him and his Spicy Pepper Penne clear-cut winners.

PIT STOP

The driver roars his car into the pit. Every millisecond counts. Strategy and skill mean valuable time and position.

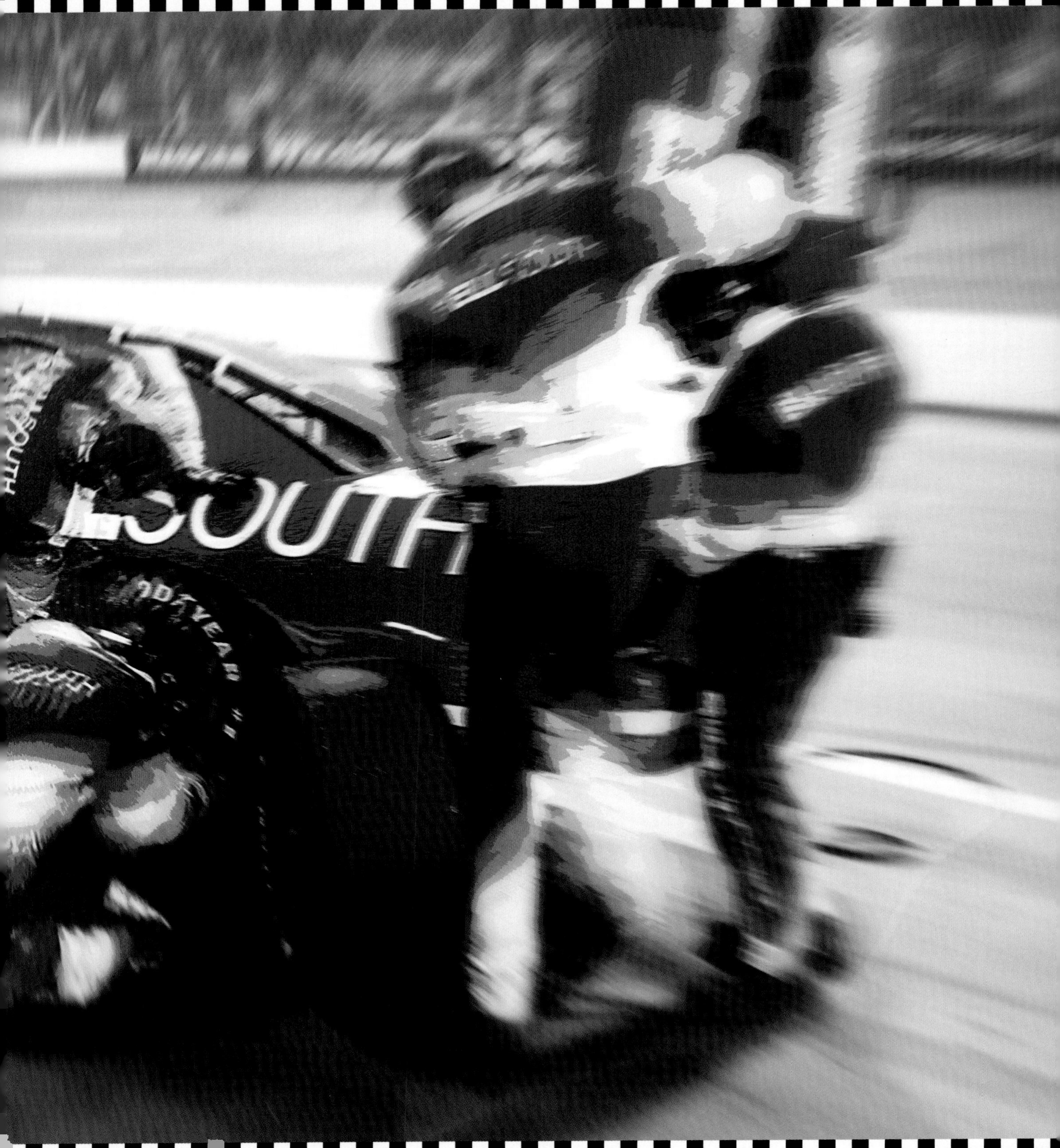

Greg Penske's
Grilled Swordfish Steaks

2 lemons

3 pounds swordfish or bluefish steaks, about 1 inch thick

1/4 cup mayonnaise

1 teaspoon TABASCO® brand Pepper Sauce

Butter or margarine, softened (optional)

3 tablespoons chopped fresh parsley

Preheat grill. Cut one lemon in half and rub both sides of steaks with lemon juice. In a small bowl, blend mayonnaise and TABASCO® Sauce and brush on both sides of steaks. Grill steaks about 6 minutes on each side, or until fish flakes easily when tested with a fork. Remove from grill and spread with butter, if desired. Sprinkle with parsley. Cut remaining lemon into wedges and serve with fish. Makes 6 servings.

Penske. The name is everywhere—on cars, billboards, jackets, caps. And that's where Greg Penske is, everywhere his favorite sport is. He's the son of Roger Penske, one of the most famous car owners in racing history, and just like his father, Greg lives up to his reputation for being a true gentleman, treating everyone with the utmost respect.

Greg has been eating, sleeping, and breathing racing since he had the chance, as a kid, to watch former NASCAR Winston Cup champion Bobby Allison's pit crew in action. Now, as president of Penske Motorsports, he has realized his dream, overseeing the development and construction of the dynamic California Speedway. The former all-American soccer and lacrosse player keeps his pulse on motorsports by entertaining race fans, serving hot and zesty Grilled Swordfish Steaks.

Joe Nemechek's Chicken and Shrimp Mixed Grill

1 pound medium shrimp, peeled and deveined

²/₃ cup white wine vinegar

¹/₂ cup soy sauce

2 tablespoons minced fresh ginger

2 tablespoons olive oil

2 tablespoons sesame oil

2 teaspoons TABASCO® brand Garlic Pepper Sauce blend

2 large cloves garlic, minced

2 green onions, sliced

4 boneless, skinless chicken breast halves

Place shrimp on skewers. (If using wooden skewers, soak in water while preparing marinade.) In a 13x9x2-inch baking dish, combine vinegar, soy sauce, ginger, olive oil, sesame oil, TABASCO® Sauce, garlic, and green onions; mix well. Place chicken breasts and skewered shrimp in mixture; toss to coat well. Cover and refrigerate at least 2 hours and up to 24 hours, turning occasionally. Preheat grill. Grill chicken 5 to 6 inches above medium heat for 6 minutes, or until tender and no longer pink, turning once and brushing with marinade occasionally; grill shrimp 3 to 4 minutes or until pink, turning once. Makes 4 servings.

After a successful short-track career in Florida, Joe Nemechek moved to North Carolina and joined the NASCAR Busch Series. In 1992, he was named the tour's most popular driver, and he returned the next season to win the NASCAR Busch Series title, while maintaining his relationship with the fans with his second consecutive most popular driver award. Joe has since moved

to the NASCAR Winston Cup tour where, in 1997, he earned the nickname "Front Row Joe" after five times qualifying in one of the top two spots.

When Joe breaks away from racing, you'll find him boating, fishing, or snow-skiing with his wife Andrea. Naturally, he plays just as hard as he races, and after a day outdoors, he takes pride in preparing his Chicken and Shrimp Mixed Grill. It's one tasty reward everyone will enjoy, even his competitors.

Ernie Irvan's Lemon-Garlic Grilling Sauce

1/4 cup butter, melted

1/4 cup olive oil

1/4 cup lemon juice

1 tablespoon Worcestershire sauce

1 tablespoon TABASCO® brand Green Pepper Sauce

3 cloves garlic, minced

In a small bowl, combine all ingredients and blend well. Brush on fish, seafood, poultry, or vegetables during grilling or broiling. Heat any remaining sauce and serve with grilled foods. Makes about 3/4 cup.

Guts, stamina, humor, determination. The name is Ernie Irvan, or it could just as well be courage. Irvan's the comeback kid who wins great respect everywhere he goes.

Ernie turned heads on the short tracks of California and North Carolina before working his way into NASCAR Winston Cup, where he won the 1991

Daytona 500. Irvan's career was halted for more than a year after suffering injuries in 1994, and that's where the courage kicked in. Thanks to the strong support of his wife Kim, daughter Jordan, teammates, and thousands of fans, he made a swift comeback to racing in 1995, winning twice one year later.

His fire is hotter than ever! Ernie's spicy Lemon-Garlic Grilling Sauce earns him as much respect at a barbecue as his skills behind the wheel.

Kyle Petty's Spicy Thai Chicken

³/₄ cup canned cream of coconut

3 tablespoons lime juice

3 tablespoons soy sauce

8 sprigs fresh cilantro

3 large cloves garlic, minced

3 green onions, coarsely chopped

3 anchovy fillets

1 teaspoon TABASCO® brand Pepper Sauce

4 boneless, skinless chicken breast halves (about 1¹/₂ pounds)

Combine cream of coconut, lime juice, soy sauce, cilantro, garlic, green onions, anchovies, and TABASCO® Sauce in container of food processor or blender and process until smooth. Place chicken in a shallow dish and pour marinade over chicken; cover and refrigerate at least 2 hours, turning chicken occasionally. Preheat grill. Remove chicken from marinade and grill 4 to 6 inches from heat for 5 minutes. Brush chicken with marinade and turn; cook 5 minutes longer or until chicken is no longer pink. Pour any remaining marinade into a small saucepan and bring to a boil; reduce heat to low and simmer 5 minutes. Serve as a dipping sauce with chicken. Makes 4 servings.

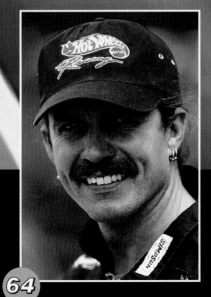

What do you do when your father is Richard Petty and your grandfather is the legendary Lee Petty? You keep your eye on Victory Lane!

Kyle Petty, the only third-generation driver to win a NASCAR Winston Cup race, is one of the more popular drivers on the tour. Despite being just 37 years old, Kyle already has started in more than 500 races in his NASCAR

Winston Cup career, during which he has won eight times.

Off the track, Kyle is an accomplished spokesman and guitar player. He also spends much of his free time working with charities, which twice has earned him NASCAR True Value Man of the Year nominations.

Kyle's clan includes his wife, Patti, and his kids, Montgomery, Austin, and Adam.

So sit back, hum your favorite tune, and enjoy Kyle's Spicy Thai Chicken. It's a tough act to follow.

Bobby Labonte's Grilled Rosemary Flank Steak

$^1/_2$ **cup steak sauce**

1 large shallot, minced, or 2 tablespoons minced onion

1 clove garlic, minced

1 tablespoon vegetable oil

1 tablespoon chopped fresh rosemary or 2 teaspoons dried

1 teaspoon TABASCO® brand Pepper Sauce

1 (2-pound) beef flank steak, trimmed

Rosemary sprigs (optional)

In a 12x8x2-inch baking dish, combine steak sauce, shallot, garlic, oil, rosemary, and TABASCO® Sauce; mix well. Add flank steak; turn to coat both sides. Cover and refrigerate at least 2 hours or overnight. Bring to room temperature before grilling. Preheat grill. Grill steak over medium heat for 12 to 15 minutes for medium-rare, or until desired doneness, turning midway. Serve with additional steak sauce and garnish with rosemary sprigs, if desired. Makes 6 to 8 servings.

It's a rare occasion when you can compete with your brother in the same race and both come out winners! That's just what Bobby Labonte and his brother Terry did in Atlanta in the final race of 1996. Bobby won the race and Terry was crowned the NASCAR Winston Cup champion.

Bobby now calls North Carolina home, but his heart is as big as his home state of Texas. And so is his spicy Grilled Rosemary Flank Steak.

Jeremy Mayfield's Kentucky Burgoo

2½ pounds chicken, cut up

1 pound beef shank bones

1 pound lean beef or pork, cut into 1-inch cubes

½ pound lean lamb, cut into 1-inch cubes

1 large potato, peeled and diced

1 large onion, chopped

2 carrots, peeled and sliced

2 cups diced tomatoes

1 bell pepper, diced

1 cup sliced celery

1 cup fresh or frozen lima beans

1 cup chopped cabbage

1 cup fresh or frozen sliced okra

1 cup fresh or frozen corn kernels

2 tablespoons vinegar or lemon juice

1½ tablespoons TABASCO® brand Pepper Sauce

Salt and pepper to taste

Place chicken and meat in a large Dutch oven and cover with water. Bring to a boil, reduce heat, and simmer at least 2 hours. Lift out chicken and remove skin and bones; shred chicken and meat. Skim fat from surface of broth and return meat and chicken to broth. Add vegetables and remaining ingredients to pot and bring to a boil. Reduce heat and simmer at least 2 more hours, stirring occasionally and adding additional water if stew gets too thick. Makes 8 to 10 servings.

Jeremy got a jump start racing go-carts and since then has driven practically every kind of car imaginable. That's what rocketed him right into the NASCAR Winston Cup Series

His wife, Christina, says that off the circuit, Jeremy's still a man with a mission, especially when he serves his hometown specialty, Kentucky Burgoo.

Ron Hornaday's TABASCO®-Seared Burgers

1   pound lean ground beef

1   small onion, finely chopped

2   tablespoons chopped fresh parsley

1   tablespoon steak sauce

2   teaspoons TABASCO® brand Pepper Sauce, divided

³/₄ teaspoon salt

1   tablespoon butter or margarine, melted

4   hamburger buns, split

Lettuce leaves

Tomato slices

Preheat grill. In a large bowl, combine ground beef, onion, parsley, steak sauce, 1 teaspoon of TABASCO® Sauce, and salt; mix well. Shape mixture into four ¹/₂-inch-thick patties. Combine butter and remaining 1 teaspoon TABASCO® Sauce; brush on burgers. Grill burgers 4 to 6 inches from heat for 3 to 4 minutes on each side or until cooked to desired doneness. To serve, place lettuce and tomato on buns and top with burger. Makes 4 servings.

Ron Hornaday, Jr., won a championship in his first year racing go-carts. A few years later he got a call from seven-time NASCAR Winston Cup champion, Dale Earnhardt, to drive in the NASCAR Craftsman Truck Series. Sure enough, a year later, Ron brought home the series' championship.

True to Ron's driving—look out for his spicy TABASCO®-Seared Burgers.

T. Wayne Robertson's Firecracker Grilled Corn on the Cob

1 cup unsalted butter or margarine, softened

2 teaspoons TABASCO® brand Pepper Sauce

8 ears corn on the cob, unshucked

Preheat grill. In a small bowl, combine butter and TABASCO® Sauce; mix well. Peel back one side of corn husk from each ear of corn without removing completely; loosen remaining husks, but do not remove silk. Brush butter mixture over corn kernels and smooth back husk to original shape. Place corn directly onto coals. Cover grill with lid or foil tent and cook 2 to 3 minutes, or until corn is done. Outsides of husks will be charred. Makes 8 servings.

T. Wayne Robertson's job as president of RJR's Sports Marketing Enterprises is to oversee the sports marketing efforts for R.J. Reynolds and Winston. That means reviewing everything regarding his company's sponsorship role in the NASCAR Winston Cup, NASCAR Winston West, and NASCAR Winston Racing Series.

T. Wayne's favorite? This Firecracker Grilled Corn on the Cob.

69

RIDING THE WALL

Sometimes making it to Victory Lane means making a move and finding room where there doesn't appear to be any.

Patti Wheeler's Risotto with Vegetables

1 small red bell pepper

1½ tablespoons butter or margarine

1½ tablespoons olive oil

1 cup sliced mushrooms

½ cup chopped onion

1 clove garlic, minced

1 cup uncooked Arborio rice

2 cups hot chicken broth, divided

½ teaspoon TABASCO® brand Pepper Sauce

Pinch saffron (optional)

1 to 1½ cups hot water, divided

1 (9-ounce) package frozen artichoke hearts, cooked and drained

Place bell pepper on a fork and carefully hold over stove burner until pepper skin blisters. Cool slightly, then peel and coarsely chop; set aside. Heat butter and oil in a large skillet over medium heat. Add mushrooms, onion, and garlic; cook 5 minutes or until onion is translucent, stirring often. Stir in rice and cook 1 to 2 minutes or until partly translucent, stirring often. Add ½ cup of the hot broth, the TABASCO® Sauce, and saffron, if desired; stir constantly until rice absorbs broth. Add remaining broth and hot water ½ cup at a time, stirring constantly and waiting until all liquid is absorbed before adding more. Cook and stir until rice is tender but firm to the bite, and risotto is consistency of creamy rice pudding, about 30 minutes total cooking time. Stir in artichokes and roasted peppers. Serve with additional TABASCO® Sauce, if desired. Makes 6 servings.

As a teenager, Patti Wheeler was a broadcast intern at Charlotte Motor Speedway—a track run by her father, H.A. "Humpy" Wheeler.

Her passion for stock cars and television led her to filming documentaries and races. Today she's president of WorldSports Enterprises, a production company for race events and news magazines—she also produces this Risotto with Vegetables.

Ray Hand's Bacon and Brandy Baked Beans

- 1   pound navy or pea beans
- Water
- $^1/_4$ pound thick-sliced bacon, cut into $^1/_2$-inch strips
- $^1/_2$ cup ketchup
- $^1/_2$ cup molasses
- 1   tablespoon Dijon mustard
- 1   tablespoon powdered mustard
- 1   medium onion, chopped
- $^1/_2$ cup brandy
- 2   teaspoons TABASCO® brand Pepper Sauce
- 1   teaspoon cider vinegar
- 1   teaspoon salt
- $^1/_2$ teaspoon black pepper

Wash and soak beans according to package directions. Drain beans and cover with 4 cups water; bring to a boil. Reduce heat to low, cover, and simmer 30 to 40 minutes or until beans are tender but not mushy. Drain, reserving liquid. Preheat oven to 250°F. In a bean pot or 3-quart casserole, combine beans, 1$^1/_2$ cups of reserved bean liquid, and all remaining ingredients; mix well. Cover and bake 6 hours, adding additional bean liquid or water if beans become dry. Makes 8 to 10 servings.

Ray Hand may have started his career as a pro football player, but his interest in racing has been NASCAR's good fortune. Ray was intrigued by the dedication of NASCAR teams when he got involved in the sport 15 years ago. Now, he owns several restaurants, most notably the NASCAR Cafe.

Ray's barbecues include his mighty tasty Bacon and Brandy Baked Beans.

Felix Sabates' Black Beans with Rum

- 1 **pound dried black beans**
- 1 **medium onion, sliced**
- 1 **stalk celery, chopped**
- 1 **bay leaf**
- 1/4 **teaspoon dried thyme leaves, crumbled**
- 1/4 **pound salt pork, cubed**
- 1 **teaspoon butter or margarine**
- 1 **teaspoon all-purpose flour**
- 1 **teaspoon salt**
- 1 **tablespoon TABASCO® brand Green Pepper Sauce**
- 1/4 **cup dark rum**
- **Sour cream (optional)**

Pick through beans to remove any grit or small pebbles; rinse thoroughly. Place beans in a large saucepan and add enough water to cover beans by 2 inches; soak overnight. Drain beans and cover with 5 cups water. Add onion, celery, bay leaf, thyme, and salt pork and bring to a boil. Reduce heat to low, cover, and simmer until beans are tender, about 2 to 2 1/2 hours, stirring occasionally. Drain, reserving 2 cups of bean liquid. Place beans in a 2-quart casserole.

Preheat oven to 350°F. Melt butter in a small saucepan over low heat; stir in flour, salt, TABASCO® Sauce, and reserved bean liquid. Cook and stir over medium heat until bubbly; remove from heat and stir in rum. Pour mixture over beans in casserole; mix well. Check seasoning and add additional salt, if needed. Bake uncovered for 25 to 30 minutes. Top each serving with a dollop of sour cream, if desired. Makes 12 servings.

Felix Sabates fled Cuba at the height of the revolution. After he had become a successful businessman, NASCAR racing lured his interests. Felix has built one of the most well-known multi-car race teams in the NASCAR Winston Cup Series.

Felix can spot winners, and he believes every time you race you have to believe you're going to win—just like his spicy winner, Black Beans with Rum.

Johnny Benson's Oven-Chipped Potatoes

- **4 medium-size russet potatoes, unpeeled and thinly sliced (about 1½ pounds)**
- **⅓ cup butter or margarine**
- **1 tablespoon grated onion**
- **½ teaspoon salt**
- **½ teaspoon dried oregano leaves, crumbled**
- **1 teaspoon TABASCO® brand Pepper Sauce**
- **⅛ teaspoon black pepper**
- **1½ cups shredded cheddar cheese**
- **1 tablespoon chopped fresh parsley**

Preheat oven to 425°F. Layer half of potato slices in a greased 13x9x2-inch baking dish. Melt butter in a small saucepan over medium heat; stir in onion, salt, oregano, TABASCO® Sauce, and pepper and cook 2 to 3 minutes or until onion is translucent. Brush half of butter mixture on potatoes in baking dish; layer remaining potatoes on top and brush with remaining butter mixture. Bake uncovered for 45 minutes or until potatoes are tender. Remove from oven and sprinkle with cheese and parsley. Bake 10 minutes longer or until cheese is melted. Makes 4 to 6 servings.

In 1994, Johnny Benson won the NASCAR Busch Series Rookie of the Year and then a series' championship in 1995. Moving to the NASCAR Winston Cup Series a year later, Johnny held true to form and took home the Rookie of the Year title. Benson has been a winner everywhere he's raced and so is his spicy Oven-Chipped Potatoes.

Jimmy Spencer's Curried Carrots and Raisins

1¼ pounds carrots

1   tablespoon honey

1½ teaspoons curry powder

1½ teaspoons lemon juice

1   teaspoon Dijon mustard

½ teaspoon TABASCO® brand Pepper Sauce

1½ tablespoons unsalted butter or margarine

1   teaspoon vegetable oil

1½ teaspoons brown sugar

⅓ cup raisins

Peel carrots and cut diagonally into ½-inch slices. In a saucepan fitted with a vegetable steamer, bring 1 inch of water to a boil. Place carrots in steamer, cover, and steam 10 minutes or until fork-tender. Remove from heat, uncover, and set aside. In a medium bowl, combine honey, curry powder, lemon juice, mustard, and TABASCO® Sauce; set aside. Heat butter and oil in a large skillet over medium heat until butter is melted. Add carrots and cook 2 minutes, stirring often. Add brown sugar and raisins; cook and stir 2 minutes. Stir in honey mixture and cook 2 to 3 minutes or until carrots are well glazed, stirring constantly. Makes 6 servings.

Jimmy Spencer lives up to his reputation as "Mr. Excitement," a nickname he earned during his modified-driving days in the Northeast. He won his first two NASCAR Winston Cup wins in 1994—and now with car owner Travis Carter it is only a matter of time before Spencer produces another exciting win. Jimmy serves up even more excitement with Curried Carrots and Raisins.

Clay Earles'
Spicy Cheese Bread

1   envelope active dry yeast

1/2 teaspoon granulated sugar

4 1/2 cups all-purpose flour, divided

1 1/2 cups shredded Swiss cheese

1   tablespoon chopped fresh
    rosemary or 1 teaspoon dried

2   large eggs

1   cup milk

1 1/2 teaspoons TABASCO® brand
    Pepper Sauce

In a small bowl, stir together yeast, sugar, and *1/4 cup warm water*. Let stand 5 minutes or until foamy. Meanwhile, in a large mixing bowl, combine 4 cups of flour, the cheese, rosemary, and *1 1/2 teaspoons salt;* mix well. Lightly beat eggs in another bowl; set aside 1 tablespoon egg to brush on dough later. Heat milk and TABASCO® Sauce in a small saucepan over low heat until warm (120°F to 130°F); add to flour mixture along with eggs and yeast. Beat until mixed well.

On a lightly floured surface, knead dough 5 minutes or until smooth and elastic, kneading in remaining 1/4 cup flour. Shape dough into a ball and place in a greased bowl, turning dough over to grease top. Cover with a towel and let rise in a warm place until doubled in bulk, about 1 1/2 hours. Punch down dough and cut into three equal pieces. On a lightly floured surface, roll dough into three strips about 16 inches long; braid strips together and place on a large greased cookie sheet. Cover and let rise in a warm place until almost doubled, about 30 minutes to 1 hour.

Preheat oven to 375°F. Brush braid with reserved egg and bake for 45 minutes or until loaf sounds hollow when lightly tapped. Cool on wire rack. Makes 1 large loaf.

NASCAR and Clay Earles have been a racing tradition for 50 years. Earles built the famed half-mile Martinsville Speedway in the Blue Ridge Mountains of Virginia in 1947. Today it is the oldest sanctioned track on the NASCAR Winston Cup tour.
When fans come on race weekend, you'll find Clay prepared with his Spicy Cheese Bread, which is almost as famous as his speedway.

VICTORY LANE

The checkered flag drops. There can only be one winner. Victory means celebration for crew, families, and fans.

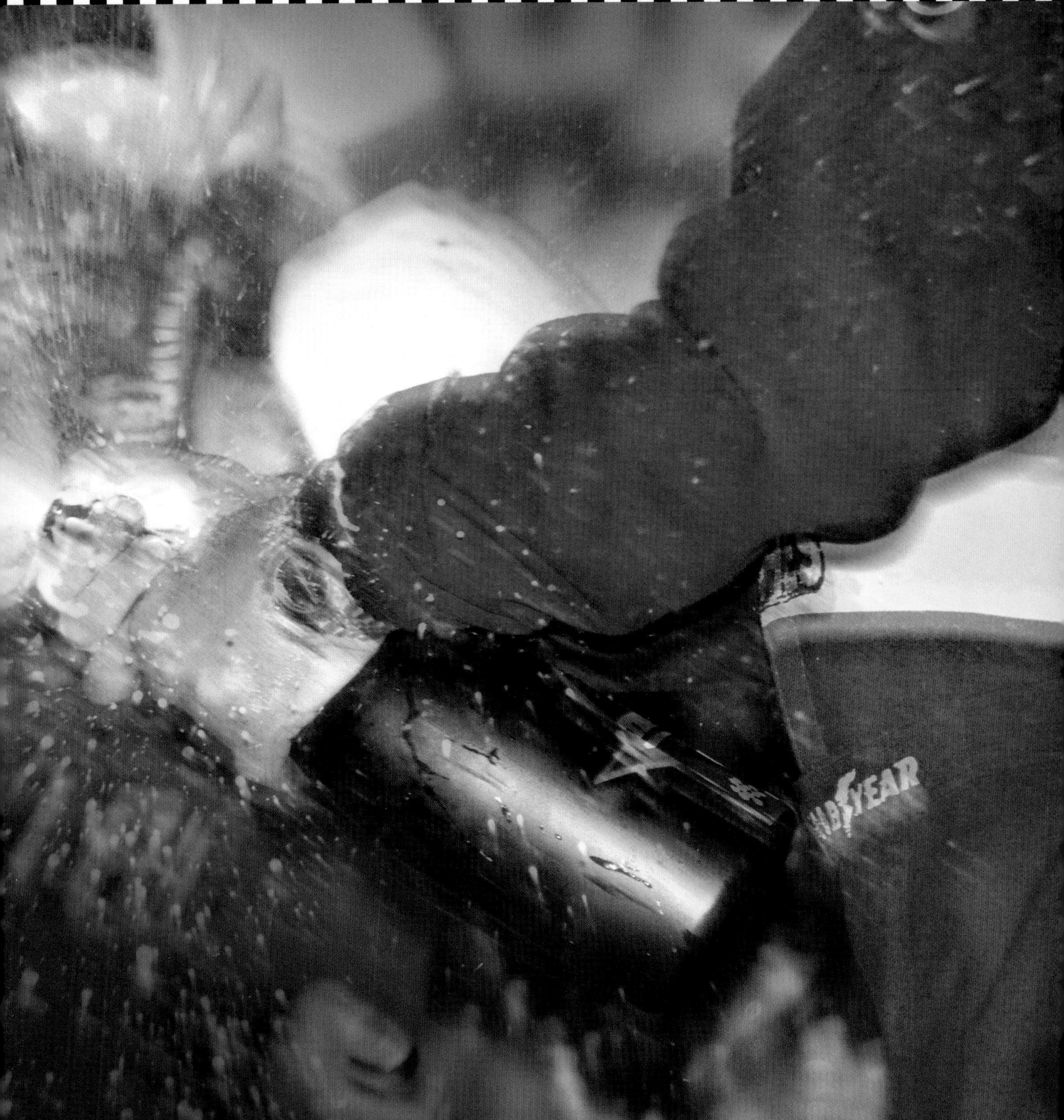

Rusty Wallace's Bloody Marys

1 quart tomato juice

1 cup vodka

1 tablespoon Worcestershire sauce

1 tablespoon fresh lime juice

½ teaspoon TABASCO® brand Pepper Sauce

Lime slices or celery stalks

In a 2-quart pitcher, combine tomato juice, vodka, Worcestershire sauce, lime juice, and TABASCO® Sauce; stir well. Pour over ice and garnish with lime or celery. Makes 6 (6-ounce) servings.

The Wallace family is a tight breed of drivers. Watching his dad race in the St. Louis area and competing with his brothers Mike and Kenny, Rusty Wallace combines both dedication and desire—which has led him to nearly 50 NASCAR Winston Cup wins and the 1989 series championship.

Relaxing for Rusty means anything from flying one of his own planes to

kicking back and listening to Garth Brooks to entertaining with his wife, Patti, three kids, and four dogs. His taste buds run as spirited and spicy as his driving style. Tell him you've got a fiesta for friends and Rusty stirs up a mighty mean classic Bloody Mary.

Cheers!

Mike McLaughlin's Zesty Bruschetta

1 baguette (about 20 to 24 inches long) French bread, cut into 1-inch slices

1 cup diced plum tomatoes, drained

1 (4-ounce) package feta cheese, crumbled (about 1 cup)

2 to 3 green onions, chopped

¼ cup chopped black olives

2 tablespoons fresh basil cut into thin strips

1 teaspoon olive oil

½ teaspoon TABASCO® brand Pepper Sauce

Salt to taste

Preheat broiler. Place bread slices on broiling pan and broil until lightly toasted on both sides; set aside. In a medium bowl, combine tomatoes, cheese, green onions, olives, basil, olive oil, TABASCO® Sauce, and salt; toss gently with a fork until blended. Mound mixture generously atop toasted bread and serve immediately. Makes 20 to 24 pieces.

Mike McLaughlin prides himself on his diverse racing background. He started building cars for others and then one day jumped into one himself. He's driven supermodifieds and dirt modifieds and moved on to win the title in NASCAR's oldest division, the Featherlite Modified tour.

He's called "Magic Shoes" for his uncanny skill of maneuvering his race

car around every track on the circuit. Mike went on to earn his first NASCAR Busch Series win in June of 1995 and followed that up with top-10 finishes in the point standings in both 1996 and 1997. It's a safe bet this native of Waterloo, New York, has some more magic on the horizon.

And taste the magic in his Zesty Bruschetta.

Richard Childress' Beer-Boiled Shrimp with Cocktail Sauce

1½ cups ketchup

2 tablespoons prepared horseradish

1 tablespoon Worcestershire sauce

2 teaspoons lemon juice

1 teaspoon TABASCO® brand Pepper Sauce

1 pound large shrimp

1 (12-ounce) bottle beer

Water

In a small bowl, combine ketchup, horseradish, Worcestershire sauce, lemon juice, and TABASCO® Sauce. Cover and refrigerate 1 hour. Peel shrimp, leaving tails intact, and devein. Pour beer into a large saucepan and add enough water to fill pan halfway; bring to a boil over high heat. Add shrimp, cover, and turn off heat. Let stand 4 minutes or until shrimp are pink; drain and rinse with cold water. Place horseradish sauce in a small bowl on a serving platter; arrange shrimp, tails down, around it. Dip shrimp in sauce. Makes 20 to 30 shrimp.

The best driver in the world is only as good as the team around him. So for the last 15 years, when teamwork and NASCAR car racing are discussed together, one name usually gets mentioned—Richard Childress.

If Childress is a top gun in the eyes of his peers, he'll certainly earn more accolades once fans chow down on his Beer-Boiled Shrimp with Cocktail Sauce.

Glen and Leonard Wood's Chicken, Beef, and Vegetable Kabobs

1 cup fresh pearl onions

¹⁄₃ cup olive oil

2 tablespoons balsamic vinegar

1 tablespoon TABASCO® brand Pepper Sauce

1 tablespoon dried basil leaves

2 large cloves garlic, crushed

1 teaspoon salt

1 pound boneless, skinless chicken breast, cut into ³⁄₄-inch chunks

1 pound boneless beef sirloin, cut into ³⁄₄-inch chunks

2 large red bell peppers, cut into ³⁄₄-inch pieces

1 large green bell pepper, cut into ³⁄₄-inch pieces

1 large zucchini, cut into ³⁄₄-inch chunks

Soak 3 dozen 4-inch-long wooden skewers in water overnight. Place onions in a 1-quart saucepan and cover with water; bring to a boil. Reduce heat to low, cover, and simmer 3 minutes or until onions are tender; drain, cool, and peel. In a medium bowl, combine olive oil, balsamic vinegar, TABASCO® Sauce, basil, garlic, and salt; mix well. Pour half of mixture into another bowl. Place chicken and beef in one bowl of marinade and toss until well coated; place onions, red and green peppers, and zucchini in remaining bowl of marinade and toss well. Cover and refrigerate for at least 30 minutes. Preheat broiler. Skewer one chunk of chicken or beef and one each of red pepper, green pepper, onion, and zucchini onto each wooden skewer. Broil 4 to 6 inches from heat, turning occasionally, for 4 to 6 minutes or until chicken and beef are done. Makes 3 dozen.

The Wood Brothers' legacy in NASCAR racing is indisputable. The drivers who have sat behind the wheels of their cars have won 95 NASCAR Winston Cup races, including four Daytona 500s.

A barbecue with the Wood Brothers is a big event. Their legendary teamwork strikes again here with these zesty Chicken, Beef, and Vegetable Kabobs.

Richard Petty's Crabmeat Squares

1 small onion, chopped

¹/₂ cup chopped celery

¹/₂ cup mayonnaise

3 eggs, beaten

1 cup evaporated milk

1 teaspoon TABASCO® brand Pepper Sauce

¹/₂ teaspoon salt

¹/₂ teaspoon black pepper

¹/₂ teaspoon prepared mustard

1 pound fresh or frozen crabmeat

¹/₂ cup butter or margarine

1 cup herb-seasoned bread stuffing mix

Preheat oven to 350°F. In a large mixing bowl, combine onion, celery, mayonnaise, eggs, milk, TABASCO® Sauce, salt, pepper, and mustard; mix well. Pick through crabmeat to remove any shell or cartilage. Gently stir crabmeat into mixture in bowl, then spoon into a greased 8-inch square baking dish.

Melt butter in a small saucepan; stir in stuffing mix and mix well. Sprinkle evenly over crabmeat filling and bake 40 minutes or until set in middle. To serve as hors d'oeuvres, cut into 2-inch squares and serve on party plates. Makes 16 hors d'oeuvres, or 6 main-dish servings.

The name is Richard Petty, and for more than 35 years he's been considered one of NASCAR's greatest legends, arguably matchless in skill and spirit. Richard certainly has earned the honor. He is an outstanding performer, and his career included seven NASCAR Winston Cup championships and 200 wins.

"The King" of stock car racing still has the competitive fire running his own NASCAR race team, which has won twice in the last two seasons. Petty still gathers a crowd wherever he goes, and a lot of times that includes his wife, four kids, and all his grandchildren when he's serving up his spicy Crabmeat Squares, which always earns more cheers!

Bob Bahre's
Elegant Cheese Ring

2   pounds grated extra-sharp cheddar cheese

1½ cups mayonnaise

2   medium onions, grated

2   tablespoons TABASCO® brand Pepper Sauce, or to taste

¾   teaspoon garlic powder

1   (12-ounce) jar strawberry preserves

Crackers

In a large bowl, combine cheese, mayonnaise, onions, TABASCO® Sauce, and garlic powder; mix very well and spoon into a well-greased 8-cup ring mold. Cover and refrigerate 24 hours to allow flavors to blend. Unmold onto a platter and fill center of ring with strawberry preserves. Serve with crackers. Makes one 8-cup ring.

Bob Bahre's a classic. He collects classic cars and builds classic race-tracks. Twenty-five years ago, he built a small, successful short track in Maine, and in 1989 he built New Hampshire International Speedway. Today, he's hosting two NASCAR Winston Cup race weekends every year.

All classics, just like his recipe for Elegant Cheese Ring.

Dr. Jerry Punch's Spinach Balls

- **2** (10-ounce) packages frozen chopped spinach
- **2** cups herb-seasoned bread stuffing mix
- **2** medium onions, finely chopped
- **1/2** cup finely chopped celery or water chestnuts
- **6** eggs, beaten
- **3/4** cup butter or margarine, melted
- **1/2** cup grated Parmesan cheese
- **1** tablespoon minced garlic
- **1** teaspoon black pepper
- **1/2** teaspoon dried thyme leaves, crumbled
- **1** teaspoon TABASCO® brand Pepper Sauce

Cook spinach according to package directions; drain very well. Meanwhile, in a large mixing bowl, combine remaining ingredients and mix well; stir in drained spinach and let stand 10 to 15 minutes to moisten stuffing mix.

Preheat oven to 350°F. Shape spinach mixture into 1-inch balls and place on a greased cookie sheet. Bake 20 minutes or until lightly browned. Makes about 5 1/2 dozen.

Jerry Punch's grandfather was a gatekeeper at Hickory Motor Speedway, so Jerry tagged along every Saturday. Even through medical school he hung around the track; then one day someone handed him the microphone.

Now as a doctor to drivers and an announcer to fans for ESPN, Jerry often prescribes his healthy Spinach Balls to spice up a winning celebration.

Andy Petree's Mushroom Quesadillas

- 2 tablespoons vegetable oil
- 8 ounces mushrooms, sliced
- 1 clove garlic, minced
- 1/4 cup chopped onion
- 1/4 cup chopped tomato
- 1 tablespoon chopped fresh cilantro
- 1 tablespoon TABASCO® brand Green Pepper Sauce
- 1/2 teaspoon salt
- 1/2 cup shredded Monterey Jack cheese
- 1/2 cup shredded cheddar cheese
- 8 corn tortillas

Preheat oven to 400°F. Heat oil in a large nonstick skillet over medium-high heat. Add mushrooms and garlic; cook 5 to 7 minutes or until mushrooms are browned and liquid is evaporated, stirring often. Add onion, tomato, cilantro, TABASCO® Sauce, and salt and cook 1 minute longer; set aside. Combine cheeses and sprinkle 2 tablespoons evenly over each of 4 tortillas; place another tortilla on top of each tortilla with cheese, and top each with an additional 2 tablespoons cheese and 2 tablespoons mushroom filling. Place quesadillas on a greased baking sheet and bake 4 to 5 minutes or until cheese is melted. Cut in half and serve immediately. Makes 16 pieces.

Andy Petree actually built his first race car from scratch. It had everything he needed to go racing, except an engine. So Dale Jarrett came along and offered to buy one for him. Honest!

After winning more than 20 races and two NASCAR Winston Cup championships, Andy is now owner and crew chief of his own NASCAR

Winston Cup team. He has become one of the most respected in the garage area while building a team as effective as the cars they produce.

His talent is evident when he serves up a hearty helping of his spicy Mushroom Quesadillas.

Bud Moore's Peppered Pecans

3   tablespoons butter or margarine

3   cloves garlic, minced

2½ teaspoons TABASCO® brand
     Pepper Sauce

½ teaspoon salt

3   cups pecan halves

Preheat oven to 250°F. Melt butter
in a small skillet; add garlic,
TABASCO® Sauce, and salt and
cook 1 minute. Toss pecans with
butter mixture; spread in a single
layer on a baking sheet. Bake
1 hour or until pecans are crisp,
stirring occasionally. Makes 3 cups.

Bud Moore won five Purple Hearts and two Bronze Stars in battle in World War II and took that same dedication and ferocity into his NASCAR racing career. As one of the most respected mechanics and car owners of all time, Moore has career records that are among the most prestigious in stock car history.

Bud began building competitive engines in 1946, and he formed his own race team in 1961. Since then, his cars and drivers have won more than 60 races, 41 poles, and the NASCAR Winston Cup championship in his extraordinary career as a car owner.

Extraordinary is also Bud's Peppered Pecans.

Recipe Index

This book is dedicated to the loving memory of T. Wayne Roberston

who was a very special person to the sport of NASCAR racing and

to each person featured in this book.

He was also a great friend to Motor Racing Outreach and the

Winston Cup Racing Wives Auxiliary who will benefit from each

purchase of NASCAR COOKS. We will miss him dearly.